MW01493930

SESMA
Children's
Bilingual
PICTURE
DICTIONARY

English - Arabic

الإنجليزية ـ العربية

Illustrations by J. Quezada
Published by Bilingual Dictionaries, Inc.

Bilingual Dictionaries, Inc.

SESMA Children's Bilingual Picture Dictionary
English-Arabic Edition
2nd Edition

Illustrations & Cover
Jose Quezada

Content & Design
Alex Sesma
Jose Quezada

Editor
C. Sesma, M.A.
Alex Sesma

Translation
C. Sesma, M.A.

Publisher
Bilingual Dictionaries, Inc.

Bilingual Dictionaries, Inc.
PO Box 1154, Murrieta, CA 92564, USA
Email: support@bilingualdictionaries.com

ISBN13: 978-0-933146-00-6 **ISBN10:** 0-933146-00-0

For information about the SESMA Picture Dictionary series and other bilingual educational materials visit:
www.BilingualDictionaries.com

SESMA Picture Dictionary

More than 1000 Illustrations

A simple bilingual picture dictionary with fun illustrations. Great for children ages 5-12.

أكثر من 1000 رسم توضيحي

قاموس صور ثنائي اللغة بسيط مع رسوم توضيحية ممتعة. مناسب للأطفال الذين تتراوح أعمارهم بين 12-5.

Lots of Languages

We are proud to publish the SESMA Picture Dictionary in many different languages from around the world. Find all our language editions online.

الكثير من اللغات

نحن فخورون ينشر قاموس صور SESMA بعدة لغات مختلفة من جميع أنحاء العالم. ابحث عن جميع إصدارات لغاتنا على الإنترنت.

Hello Привет こんにちは Ciao Bonjour ولى‌ه Sawubona 여보세요 Hola 你好 Hallo Olá

BilingualDictionaries.com

Buy Now

The new and improved SESMA Picture Dictionary is back! Purchase bilingual educational materials in over 50 languages.

اشتري الآن

قاموس صور SESMA الجديد والمحسّن! اشتري مواد تعليمية ثنائية اللغة بأكثر من 50 لغة.

Table of Contents

Table of Contents

Numbers

0	1	2	3
zero صفر	**one** واحد	**two** إثنان	**three** ثلاثة

4	5	6	7
four أربعة	**five** خمسة	**six** ستة	**seven** سبعة

8	9	10	11
eight ثمانية	**nine** تسعة	**ten** عشرة	**eleven** أحد عشرة

12	13	14	15
twelve اثني عشر	**thirteen** ثلاثة عشر	**fourteen** أربعة عشرة	**fifteen** خمسة عشر

16	17	18	19
sixteen سادس عشر	**seventeen** سبعة عشر	**eighteen** ثمانية عشرة	**nineteen** تسعة عشر

20	30	40	50
twenty عشرون	**thirty** ثلاثون	**forty** أربعون	**fifty** خمسون

60	70	80	90
sixty ستون	**seventy** سبعون	**eighty** ثمانون	**ninety** تسعون

الأعداد

Numbers

100

one hundred
مائة

1,000

one thousand
ألف

1,000,000

one million
مليون

1,000,000,000

one billion
مليار

1st

first
أول

2nd

second
ثاني

3rd

third
ثالث

4th

fourth
رابع

5th

fifth
خامس

6th

sixth
سادس

7th

seventh
سابع

8th

eighth
ثامن

9th

ninth
تاسع

10th

tenth
عاشر

11th

eleventh
حاديه عشر

12th

twelfth
ثاني عشر

13th

thirteenth
ثلث عشر

14th

fourteenth
رابع عشر

15th

fifteenth
خامس عشر

16th

sixteenth
سادس عشر

17th

seventeenth
سابع عشر

18th

eighteenth
ثامن عشر

19th

nineteenth
تاسع عشر

20th

twentieth
عشرون

Colors

purple أرجواني	black أسود
blue أزرق	white أبيض
green أخضر	gray رمادي
yellow أصفر	brown بني
orange برتقالي	tan أسمر
red أحمر	gold ذهبي
pink زهري	silver فضي

الألوان

Shapes

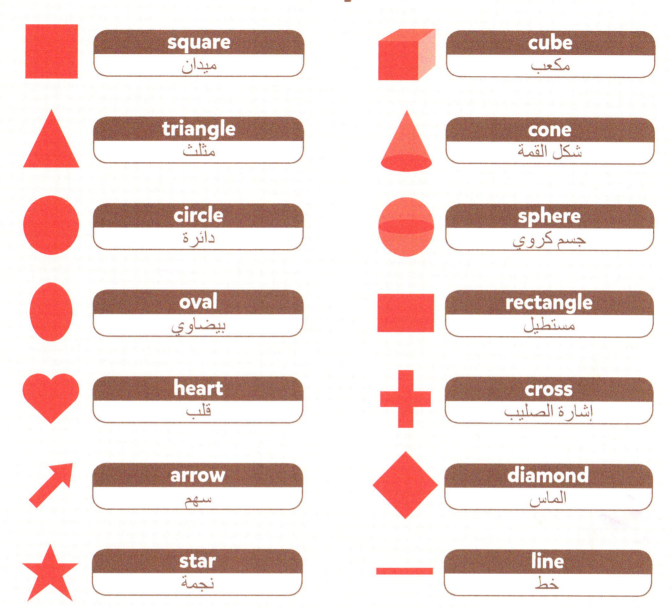

square ميدان	**cube** مكعب
triangle مثلث	**cone** شكل القمة
circle دائرة	**sphere** جسم كروي
oval بيضاوي	**rectangle** مستطيل
heart قلب	**cross** إشارة الصليب
arrow سهم	**diamond** الماس
star نجمة	**line** خط

Calendar

calendar
التقويم

date
تاريخ

month
شهر

day
يوم

year
عام

January
كانون الثاني

February
شباط

March
اذار

April
نيسان

May
ايار

June
حزيران

July
تموز

August
آب

September
أيلول

October
تشرين الأول

November
تشرين الثاني

December
كانون الأول

Calendar

SUN	MON	TUE	WED	THR	FRI	SAT

Sunday
الأحد

SUN	MON	TUE	WED	THR	FRI	SAT

Monday
الإثنين

SUN	MON	TUE	WED	THR	FRI	SAT

Tuesday
الثلاثاء

SUN	MON	TUE	WED	THR	FRI	SAT

Wednesday
الأربعاء

SUN	MON	TUE	WED	THR	FRI	SAT

Thursday
الخميس

SUN	MON	TUE	WED	THR	FRI	SAT

Friday
الجمعة

SUN	MON	TUE	WED	THR	FRI	SAT

Saturday
السبت

SUN	MON	TUE	WED	THR	FRI	SAT

week
أسبوع

SUN	MON	TUE	WED	THR	FRI	SAT

weekday
يوم من أيام الأسبوع

SUN	MON	TUE	WED	THR	FRI	SAT

weekend
عطلة نهاية الاسبوع

today
اليوم

yesterday
في الامس

tomorrow
غدا

Greetings

hello
مرحبا

goodbye
وداعا

please
رجاء

thank you
شكرا

yes
نعم

no
لا

تحية طيبة

Questions ?

who
من الذي

what
ماذا

when
متى

where
أين

why
لماذا

how
كيف

When?

time
زمن

twelve o' clock
الساعة الثانية عشر

one o' clock
الساعة الواحدة

two o'clock
الساعة الثانية

three o'clock
الساعة الثالثة

four o'clock
الساعة الرابعة

five o'clock
الساعة الخامسة

six o'clock
الساعة السادسة

seven o'clock
الساعة السابعة

eight o'clock
الساعة الثامنة

nine o'clock
الساعة التاسعة

ten o'clock
الساعة العاشرة

eleven o'clock
الساعة الحادية عشر

متى؟

When?

sunrise

شروق الشمس

noon

وقت الظهيرة

sunset

غروب الشمس

midnight

منتصف الليل

one fifteen

الساعة واحدة وخمسة عشر دقيقة

quarter past one

الساعة واحدة إلا خمسة عشر دقيقة

one thirty

الساعة واحدة وثلاثون دقيقة

half past one

الساعة واحدة ونصف

one forty-five

الساعة واحدة وخمسة وأربعين دقيقة

a quarter to two

الساعة الثانية إلا ربع

hour

ساعة

minute

دقيقة

second

ثانيا

متى؟

Where?

up فوق	**down** أسفل
left اليسار	**right** حق
top الأعلى	**bottom** الأسفل
front أمامي	**back** الى الخلف
near قريب	**far** بعيدا

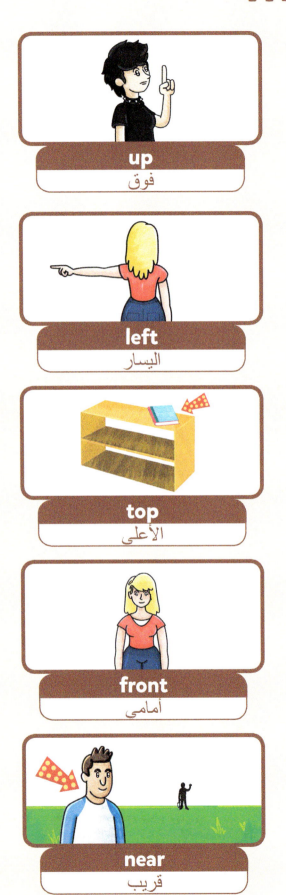
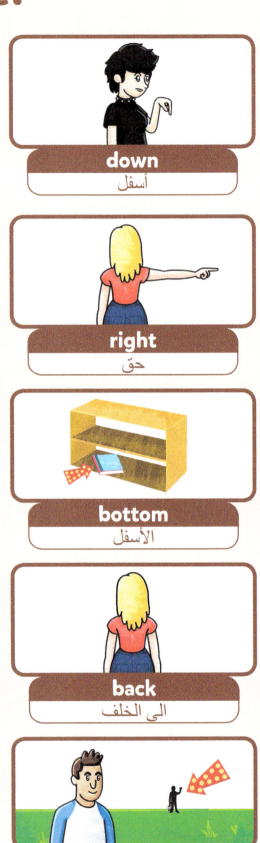

أين؟

Where?

inside
فى داخل

outside
فى الخارج

in front
امام

behind
خلف

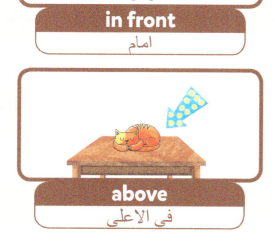

above
فى الاعلى

below
أدناه

between
ما بين

next to
بجوار

over
على

under
تحت

أين؟

17

Money (USA)

$1.00
dollar
دولار

$0.01
penny
قرش

$0.05
nickel
النيكل

$0.10
dime
عشرة سنتات

$0.25
quarter
عشرة سنتات

$0.66
sixty-six cents
ستة وستون سنتا

$0.33
thirty-three cents
ثلاثة وثلاثين سنتا

$1.26
one dollar and twenty-six cents
دولار واحد وستة وعشرين سنتا

المال

Chapter 1
Family

الفصل 1
العائلة

Family

1. grandmother

2. grandfather

3. aunt

4. mother

5. father

6. uncle

7. brother

8. sister

9. cousin

1. الجدة	2. الجد	3. العمة أو الخالة
4. الأم	5. الأب	6. العم أو الخال
7. الأخ	8. الأخت	9. إبن العم او الخال

العائلة

Family

1. parents

2. children

3. husband and wife

4. son and daughter

5. niece and nephew

1. الآباء

2. الأولاد

3. الزوج والزوجة

4. الإبن والإبنة

5. إبن وإبنة الأخ أو الأخت

العائلة

Family • Age

1. baby	2. child	3. teenager

4. adult	5. senior	6. woman
	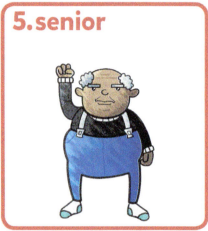	

7. girl	8. boy	9. man

3. مراهق	2. ولد	1. طفل
6. إمرأة	5. مسنّ	4. راشد
9. رجل	8. صبيّ	7. فتاة

العائلة • العمر

Family • Description

1. handsome

2. pretty

3. ugly

4. skinny

5. tall

6. young

7. fat

8. short

9. old

3.قبيح	2.وسيم	1. وسيم
6.يافع	5.طويل	4.نحيف
9.عجوز	8.قصير	7. سمين

العائلة • الوصف

Family • Birthday

1. birthday

2. cake

3. candle

4. balloon

5. gift

6. party

7. friend

8. game

9. fun

3. شمعة	2. كعكة	1. عيد الميلاد
6. حفلة	5. هدية	4. بالون
9. مرح	8. لعبة	7. صديق

العائلة • عيد الميلاد

Family • Wedding

1. wedding

2. bride

3. groom

4. to cry

5. to dance

6. to laugh

7. to love

8. to kiss

9. to hug

3. عريس	2. عروس	1. عرس
6. يضحك	5. يرقص	4. تبكي
9. يعانق	8. يقبّل	7. يحبّ

Family • Emotions

1. happy

2. sad

3. scared

4. angry

5. surprised

6. excited

7. embarrassed

8. proud

9. shy

1. سعيد	2. حزين	3. خائف
4. غاضب	5. مندهش	6. متحمس
7. متحمس	8. فخور	9. خجول

العائلة • العواطف

Chapter 2
Home

الفصل 2
البيت

Home

1.house 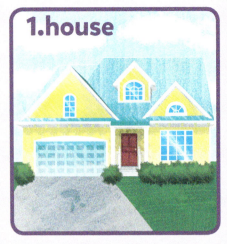	**2.apartment** 	**3.door** 
4.window 	**5.doorknob** 	**6.doorbell** 
7.key 	**8.to knock** 	**9.to ring** 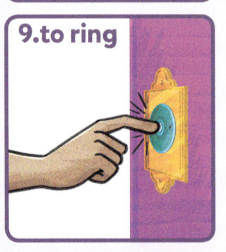

3.باب	2.شقة	1.بيت
6.جرس الباب	5.مقبض الباب	4.نافذة
9.يرنّ	8.يقرع	7.مفتاح

البيت

Home

1.stairs 	2.roof 	3.chimney 
4.gate 	5.garage 	6.fence 
7.mailbox 	8.mail 	9.to receive 

3.مدخنة	2.سقف	1.الدرج
6.سياج	5.مرأب	4.بوابة
9.يتلقى	8.بريد	7.صندوق البريد

البيت

Home

1. kitchen

2. bedroom

3. bathroom

4. living room

5. yard

1. مطبخ

2. غرفة النوم

3. حمام

4. غرفة الجلوس

5. حديقة

البيت

Home

1. neighbor

2. to meet

Hello!

3. to invite

You're invited!

4. to wave

5. to play

1. جار

2. يلتقي

3. يدعو

4. يلوّح

5. يلعب

البيت

31

Home • Kitchen

1.refrigerator

2.dishwasher

3.microwave

4.toaster

5.stove

6.oven

7.sink

8.counter

9.cupboard

3.ميكروويف	2.غسالة صحون	1.ثلاجة
6.فرن	5.موقد	4.محمصة خبز كهربائية
9.خزانة صحون	8.منضدة	7.حوض

البيت • المطبخ

Home • Kitchen

1.plate

2.bowl

3.cup

4.knife

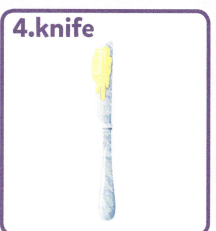

5.fork

6.spoon

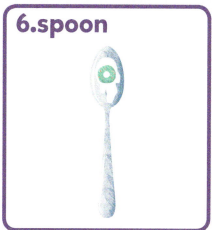

7.table

8.chair

9.napkin

3.كوب	2.وعاء	1.طبق
6.ملعقة	5.شوكة	4.سكين
9.منديل	8.كرسي	7.طاولة

البيت • المطبخ

Home • Bedroom

1.bed 	**2.pillow** 	**3.blanket** 
4.dresser 	**5.nightstand** 	**6.lamp** 
7.closet 	**8.poster** 	**9.light** 

1.سرير	2.وسادة	3.بطانية
4.خزانة	5.منضدة	6.مصباح
7.خزانة	8.ملصق	9.ضوء

البيت • غرفة النوم

Home • Bedroom

1. dream

2. nightmare

3. tired

4. awake

1. حلم

2. كابوس

3. متعب

4. مستيقظ

5. ينام

5. to sleep

Home • Bathroom

1.shower

2.bathtub

3.faucet

4.mirror

5.toilet

6.toilet paper

7.hamper

8.comb

9.soap

3.حنفية	2.حوض الإستحمام	1.دش
6.ورق التواليت	5.حمام	4.مرآة
9.صابون	8.مشط	7.سلة ملابس

البيت • الحمام

Home • Bathroom

1.toothbrush

2.toothpaste

3.towel

4.floss

5.wet

6.dry

7.lotion

8.clean

9.dirty

3.منشفة	2.معجون الأسنان	1.فرشاة
6.جاف	5.مبلل	4.خيط
9.قذر	8.نظيف	7.كريم

Home • Bathroom

1. to open

2. to close

3. to comb

4. to brush

5. to shower

1. يفتح

2. يقفل

3. يمشط

4. ينظف

5. يستحم

البيت • الحمام

Home • Living Room

1.wall

2.floor

3.ceiling

4.couch

5.carpet

6.outlet

7.fireplace

8.painting

9.switch

سقف.3	أرضية.2	حائط.1
مخرج.6	سجادة.5	أريكة.4
مفتاح كهربائي.9	لوحة.8	مدفأة.7

Home • Living Room

1.television

2.tablet

3.screen

4.remote

5.video game

6.board game

7.toy

8.off

9.on

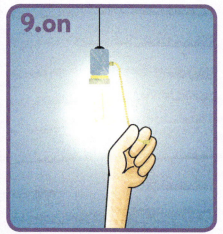

شاشة.3	لوح.2	تلفاز.1
لعبة اللوحة.6	لعبة الفيديو.5	التحكم عن بعد.4
تشغيل.9	إطفاء.8	لعبة.7

البيت • غرفة الجلوس

Home • Living Room

1. together

2. alone

3. to watch

4. to cheer

5. comfortable

1. سويا

2. وحيد

3. يشاهد

4. يهتف

5. مريح

Home • Yard

1.lawn

2.garden

3.barbecue

4.lawn mower

5.trash

6.hose

7.dog house

8.tree house

9.sprinkler

1.عشب	2.حديقة	3.الشواء
4.آلة جز العشب	5.قمامة	6.خرطوم المياه
7.بيت الكلب	8.عزال	9.مرشة

البيت • حديقة

Home • Garage

1. paint

2. ladder

3. cooler

4. fan

5. box

6. bag

7. to lift

8. to carry

9. to fall

1.طلاء	2.سلم	3.ثلاجة
4.مروحة	5.صندوق	6.كيس
7.يرفع	8.يحمل	9.يسقط

البيت • المرآب

Home • Tool

1.hammer

2.nail

3.screwdriver

4.power drill

5.toolbox

6.wrench

7.tape

8.to break

9.to fix

3.مفك براغي	2.مسمار	1.مطرقة
6.مفتاح الربط	5.صندوق الأدوات	4.حافر كهربائي
9.يصلح	8.يكسر	7.شريط لاصق

البيت • الأدوات

Home • Clean

1.broom

2.dustpan

3.mop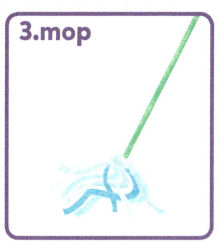

4.sponge

5.vacuum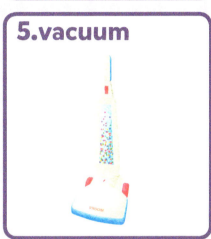

6.bucket

7.cleaner

8.duster

9.paper towel

3.ممسحة	2.مجرود	1.مكنسة
6.دلو	5.مكنسة كهربائية	4.إسفنجة
9.منشفة ورقية	8.خرقة	7.منظف

Home • Clean

1. to spray

2. to wipe

3. to sweep

4. to scrub

5. to clean

1. يرش
2. يمسح
3. يكنس
4. يفرك
5. ينظف

Chapter 3
Clothes

الفصل 3
الملابس

Clothes

1. shirt

2. pants

3. shorts

4. underwear

5. sock

6. shoes

7. sweater

8. jacket

9. hat

3. سراويل قصيرة	2. بنطال	1. قميص
6. حذاء	5. جورب	4. ثياب داخلية
9. قبعة	8. سترة	7. كنزة

الملابس

Clothes

1. sandals	2. boots	3. sneakers
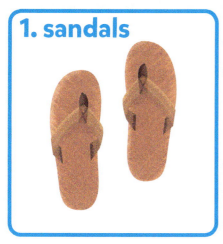		

4. heel	5. sole	6. shoelace

7. to tie	8. to put on	9. to take off

3. حذاء رياضي	2. جزمة	1. صندل
6. رباط الحذاء	5. باطن القدم	4. كعب
9. يخلع	8. يرتدي	7. يربط

Clothes • Girls

1. dress

2. skirt

3. bikini

4. make-up

5. purse

1. فستان

2. تنورة

3. بيكيني

4. ماكياج

5. محفظة

الملابس • الفتيات

Clothes • Boys

1. jeans

2. t-shirt

3. baseball cap

4. swimming trunks

5. wallet

1. جينز
2. تي شيرت
3. قبعة البيسبول
4. سراويل السباحة
5. محفظة النقود

الملابس • الصبيان

Clothes • Accessories

1. belt

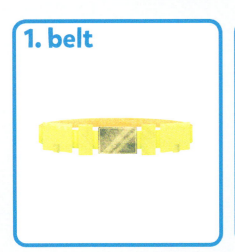

2. scarf

3. watch

4. ring

5. necklace

6. earring

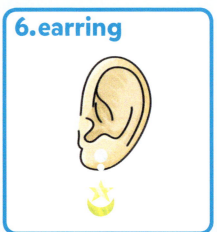

7. bracelet

8. cowboy hat

9. glove

3. ساعة	2. وشاح	1. حزام
6. حلق الأذن	5. قلادة	4. خاتم
9. قفاز	8. قبعة رعاة البقر	7. سوار

الملابس • إكسسوارات

Clothes - Accessories

1. pocket

2. sleeve

3. collar
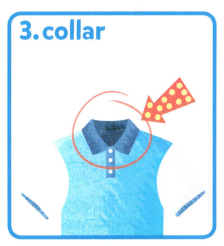

4. hood

5. zipper
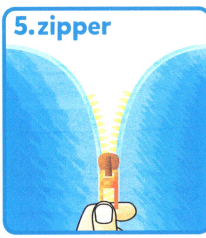

6. button

7. buckle

8. patch

9. logo

3.طوق	2.كم	1. جيب
6.زر	5.سحاب	4.قبعة السترة
9.شعار	8.رقعة	7.مشبك

الملابس • إكسسوارات

Clothes • Style

1. solid

2. striped

3. polka dot

4. small

5. medium

6. torn

7. large

8. extra-large

9. stained

1. صلب	2. مخطط	3. منقط
4. صغير	5. متوسط	6. ممزق
7. كبير	8. كبير جدا	9. ملطخ

الملابس • النمط

Clothes · Style

1. new

2. used

3. tight
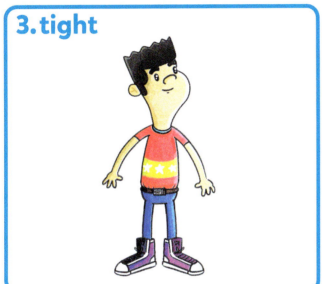

4. loose

5. style

1. جديد

2. مستخدم

3. ضيق

4. واسع

5. موضة

Clothes • Laundry

1. washer

2. dryer

3. detergent

4. basket

5. laundry

6. hanger

7. iron

8. wrinkle

9. crease

3. منظف	2. آلة تجفيف الملابس	1. غسّالة
6. أداة التعليق	5. غسيل	4. سلة
9. تجعد	8. تجعد	7. مكواة

الملابس • غسيل الملابس

Clothes • Laundry

1. to try

2. to wear

3. to fold

4. to put

5. to hang

1. يجرب
2. يرتدي
3. يطوي
4. يضع
5. يعلّق

Clothes

1. uniform

2. costume

3. pajamas

4. suit

5. robe

1. زي موحد

2. زي

3. بيجامة

4. بدلة

5. رداء

الملابس

Chapter 4
Food

الفصل 4
الطعام

Food

1. fruit

2. vegetable

3. meat

4. bread

5. condiment

1. فاكهة

2. خضار

3. لحم

4. خبز

5. توابل

الطعام

Food

1. breakfast

2. lunch

3. dinner

4. beverage

5. dessert

1. الفطور

2. الغداء

3. العشاء

4. مشروبات

5. الحلوى

Food · Fruit

1. apple

2. banana

3. grapes
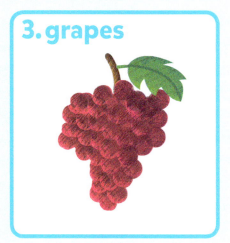

4. pineapple

5. strawberry

6. watermelon

7. pumpkin

8. avocado

9. blueberry

1. تفاحة	2. موز	3. عنب
4. أناناس	5. فراولة	6. بطيخ
7. يقطين	8. أفوكادو	9. عنب بري

الطعام • الفاكهة

Food • Fruit

1. raisin

2. orange

3. mango

4. coconut

5. lemon

6. lime

7. cherry

8. juicy

9. sour

3.مانجو	2.برتقال	1. زبيب
6.حامض	5.ليمون	4.جوز الهند
9.حامض	8.كثير العصير	7. كرز

الطعام • الفاكهة

Food • Vegetable

1. lettuce

2. celery

3. carrot

4. tomato

5. onion

6. cucumber

7. mushroom

8. broccoli

9. pickle

1. خس	2. كرفس	3. جزرة
4. طماطم	5. بصلة	6. خيار
7. فطر	8. بروكلي	9. مخلل

الطعام • الخضار

Food • Vegetable

1. asparagus

2. corn

3. potato

4. chili pepper

5. garlic

6. peas

7. rotten

8. ripe

9. fresh

1. نبات الهليون   2. حبوب ذرة   3. البطاطس

4. فلفل حار   5. ثوم   6. بازيلاء

7. فاسد   8. ناضج   9. طازج

Food • Breakfast

1. egg

2. bacon

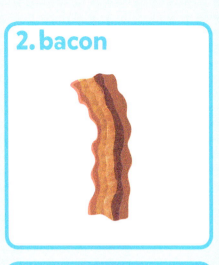

3. sausage

4. ham

5. pancakes

6. toast

7. cereal

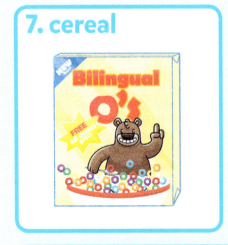

8. butter

9. syrup

3.سجق	2.لحم خنزير مقدد	1. بيض
6.خبز محمص	5.فطائر	4.لحم خنزير
9.شراب مركز	8.زبدة	7. حبوب

الطعام • الفطور

Food • Lunch

1. hamburger

2. fries

3. hotdog

4. chicken nugget

5. pizza

6. fish stick

7. sandwich

8. peanut butter

9. jelly

3.نقانق	2.بطاطا مقلية	1.هامبورغر
6.أصابع السمك	5.بيتزا	4.قطع الدجاج المقلية
9.هلام	8.زبدة الفول السوداني	7. شطيرة

Food • Lunch

1. ketchup

2. mustard

3. mayonnaise

4. salt

5. cheese

6. lunch box

7. snack

8. spicy

9. sweet

1. كاتشب	2. خردل	3. مايونيز
4. ملح	5. جين	6. صندوق الغداء
7. وجبات خفيفة	8. حار	9. حلو

الطعام • الغداء

Food • Dinner

1. steak

2. chicken

3. pasta

4. soup

5. salad

6. salad dressing

7. beans

8. rice

9. sushi

3. معكرونة	2. دجاج	1. شريحة لحم
6. صلصة السلطة	5. سلطة	4. حساء
9. سوشي	8. أرز	7. فاصولياء

الطعام • العشاء

Food • Dessert

1. candy	2. chips	3. cookie

4. donut	5. pie	6. cupcake

7. frosting	8. ice cream	9. chocolate

3. بسكويت	2. رقائق	1. حلويات
6. كعكة صغيرة	5. فطيرة	4. كعكة محلاة
9. شوكولاتة	8. مثلجات	7. كريمة الزبدة

الطعام • الحلوى

Food • Beverage

1. juice

2. milk

3. soda

4. tea

5. coffee

6. water

7. ice

8. empty

9. full

3. مشروب غازي	2. حليب	1. عصير
6. ماء	5. قهوة	4. شاي
9. شبعان	8. فارغة	7. ثلج

Food • Cook

1. pan

2. pot

3. colander

4. spatula

5. tongs

6. ladle

7. to prepare

8. to cook

9. to wash

1. مقلاة	2. طنجرة	3. مصفاة
4. الملعقة المسطحة	5. ملقط	6. مغرفة
7. يحضّر	8. يطهو	9. يغسل

الطعام • الطهو

Food • Cook

1. to grill

2. to peel

3. to stir

4. to boil

5. to fry

6. to bake

7. to mix

8. to sprinkle

9. to heat

1. يشوي	2. يقشر	3. يحرك
4. يغلي	5. يقلي	6. يخبز
7. يخلط	8. يرش	9. يسخن

الطعام • الطهو

Food • Eat

1. to eat

2. to drink

3. to chew

4. to burp

5. to pour

6. to dip

7. hungry

8. thirsty

9. delicious

3.يمضغ	2.يشرب	1. يأكل
6.يغمس	5.يسكب	4.يتجشأ
9. لذيذ	8.عطشان	7. جائع

الطعام • تناول الطعام

Chapter 5
Health

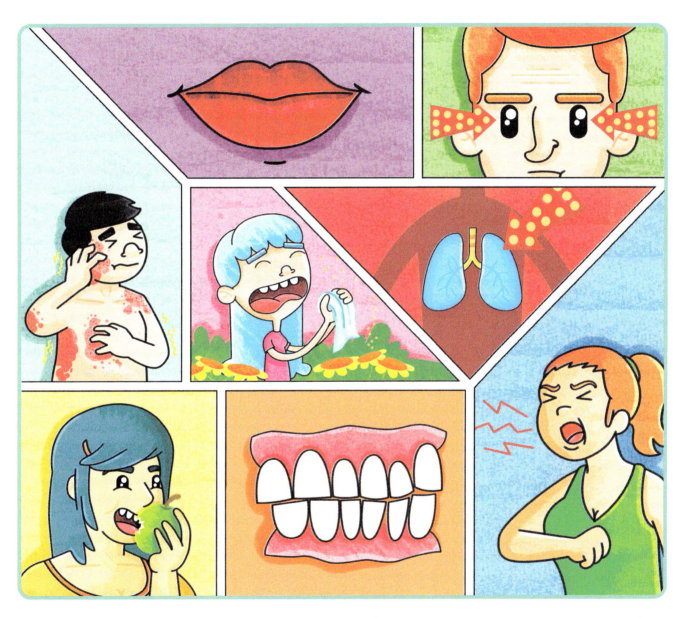

الفصل 5
الصحة

Health

1. head

2. body

3. sick

4. hurt

5. healthy

1. رأس

2. جسم

3. مريض

4. وجع

5. صحي

الصحة

Health

1. brain

2. lungs
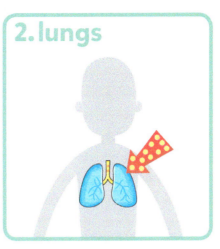

3. heart
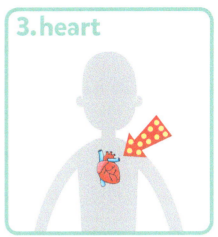

4. blood

5. skin
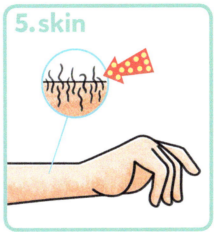

6. muscle

7. bone

8. skull

9. skeleton

3. قلب	2. رئتين	1. دماغ
6. عضلة	5. بشرة	4. دم
9. هيكل عظمي	8. جمجمة	7. عظم

الصحة

Health • Head

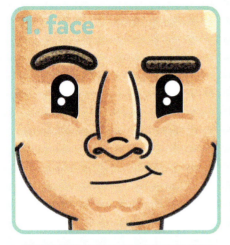
1. face

2. eye

3. nose

4. forehead

5. eyebrow

6. ear

7. cheek

8. chin

9. hair

1. وجه	2. عين	3. أنف
4. جبين	5. حاجب العين	6. أذن
7. خد	8. ذقن	9. شعر

الصحة • الرأس

Health • Head

1. mouth

2. lips

3. teeth

4. tongue

5. neck

6. to talk

7. to smile
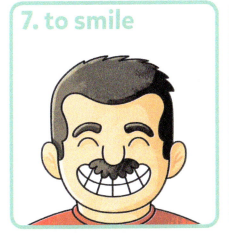

8. to bite

9. to lick

3.أسنان	2.شفاه	1. فم
6.يتكلم	5.عنق	4.لسان
9.يلعق	8.عض	7.يبتسم

Health • Body

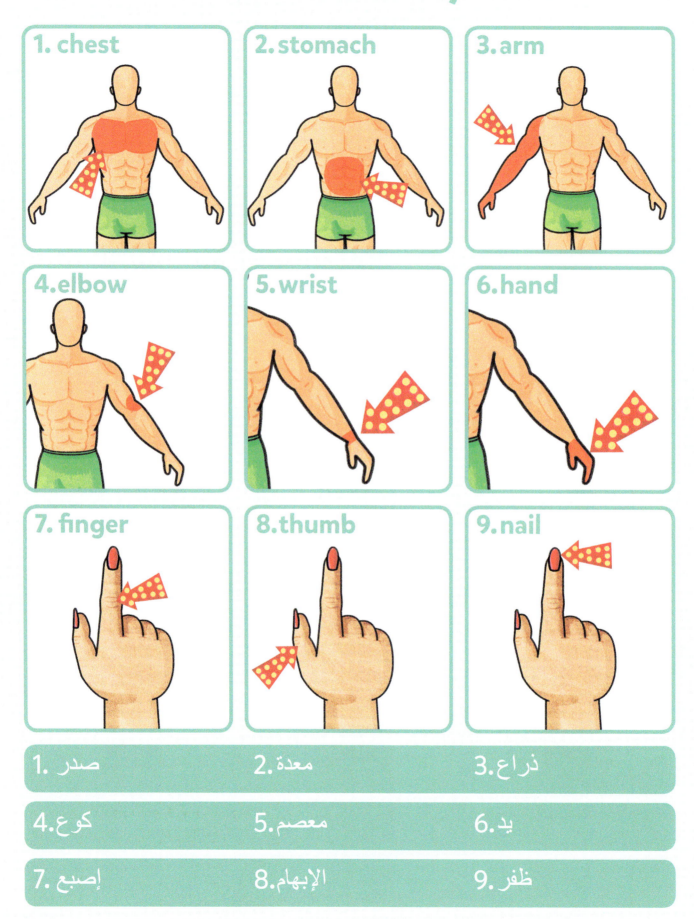

1. chest
2. stomach
3. arm
4. elbow
5. wrist
6. hand
7. finger
8. thumb
9. nail

1. صدر	2. معدة	3. ذراع
4. كوع	5. معصم	6. يد
7. إصبع	8. الإبهام	9. ظفر

الصحة • الجسم

Health • Body

1. back

2. shoulder
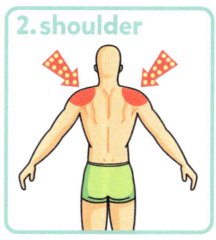

3. waist
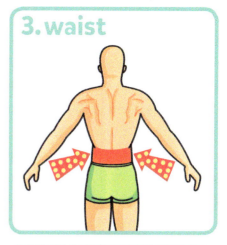

4. hips
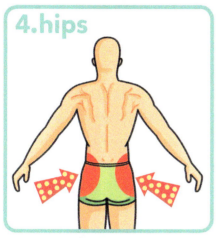

5. leg

6. knee

7. ankle
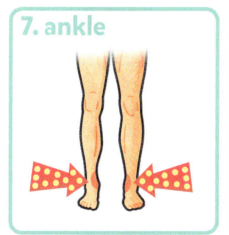

8. foot
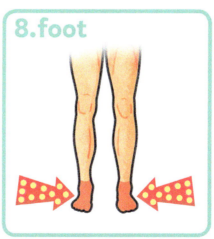

9. toe

1. ظهر	2. كتف	3. وسط
4. الفخذين	5. رجل	6. ركبة
7. كاحل	8. قدم	9. إصبع القدم

Health · Sick

1. cold

2. fever
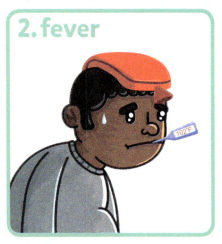

3. flu

4. headache
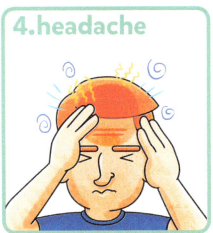

5. allergy

6. stomach ache

7. to cough

8. to sneeze

9. to vomit

1. رشح	2. حمى	3. أنفلونزا
4. صداع	5. حساسية	6. ألم المعدة
7. يسعل	8. يعطس	9. يتقيأ

الصحة · مريض

Health • Hurt

1. cut

2. bruise

3. burn

4. rash

5. bite

6. pain

7. swollen (finger)

8. broken (bone)
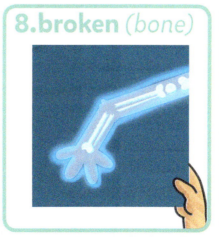

9. to bleed

1.جرح	2.كدمة	3.حرق
4.طفح جلدي	5.عضة	6.ألم
7.متورم	8.مكسور	9.ينزف

الصحة • وجع

Health • Healthy

1. to see

2. to hear

3. to taste

4. to smell

5. to touch

6. to breathe

7. to sweat

8. strong

9. weak

1. يرى	2. يسمع	3. يتذوق
4. يشم	5. يلمس	6. يتنفس
7. يتعرق	8. قوية	9. ضعيف

الصحة • صحي

Chapter 6
School

الفصل 6
المدرسة

School

1. office

2. classroom

3. cafeteria

4. field

5. auditorium

6. gym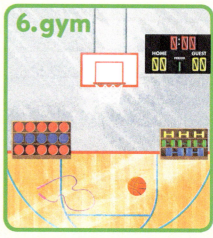

7. playground

8. restroom

9. hallway

3. كافيتيريا	2. صف	1. مكتب
6. الجمنازيوم	5. قاعة محاضرات	4. حقل
9. مدخل	8. غرفة الاستراحة	7. ملعب

المدرسة

School

1. principal
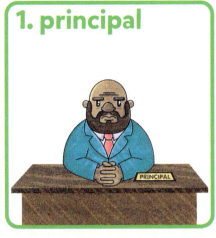

2. teacher

3. student

4. janitor

5. nurse

6. classmate

7. guard

8. fountain

9. locker

1. مدير	2. معلم	3. تلميذ
4. الناطور	5. ممرضة	6. زميل في الصف
7. حارس	8. نافورة	9. خزانة صغيرة

المدرسة

School • Classroom

1. whiteboard

2. marker

3. desk

4. projector

5. screen

6. chair

7. clock

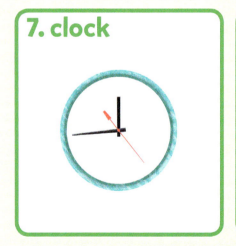

8. waste basket

9. flag

3. مكتب	2. قلم تحديد	1. لوح
6. كرسي	5. شاشة	4. جهاز عرض
9. علم	8. سلة النفايات	7. ساعة حائط

School • Classroom

1. to teach

2. to learn

3. to study

4. to think

1. يعلم

2. يتعلم

3. يدرس

4. يفكر

5. يتخرّج

5. to graduate

المدرسة • الصف

School · Math

1. math

2. odd

3. even

4. calculator

5. to add
$2+2=4$

6. to subtract
$3-1=2$

7. to multiply
$5\times2=10$

8. to divide
$8\div4=2$

9. to equal
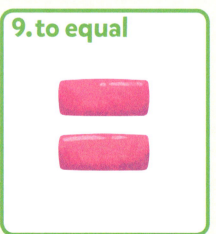

3. مزدوج	2. مفرد	1. رياضيات
6. يطرح	5. يضيف	4. آلة حاسبة
9. يساوي	8. يقسم	7. يضاعف

المدرسة · الرياضيات

School • Science

1. science

2. experiment

3. scientist

4. microscope

5. atom
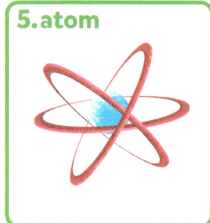

6. cell
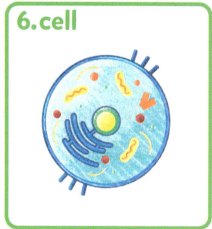

7. robot

8. electricity

9. magnet

3. عالم	2. تجربة	1. علوم
6. خلية	5. ذرة	4. مجهر
9. مغناطيس	8. كهرباء	7. إنسان آلي

المدرسة • العلوم

School • English

1. language

2. alphabet

3. letter
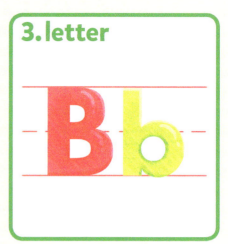

4. word

5. sentence

6. dictionary

7. to listen

8. to read

9. to write

3. حرف	2. أبجدية	1. لغة
6. قاموس	5. جملة	4. كلمة
9. يكتب	8. يقرأ	7. يصغي

المدرسة • الإنجليزية

School • Lesson

1. lesson
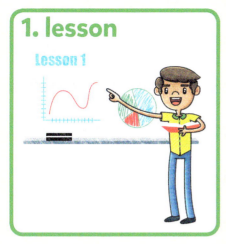

2. homework

3. test

4. question
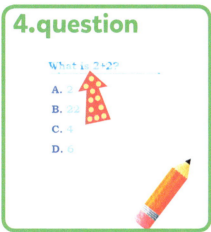

5. easy

6. difficult

7. answer
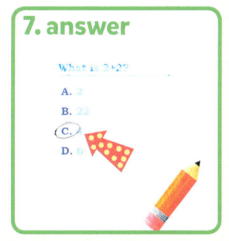

8. to remember

9. to forget

3. اختبار	2. واجب	1. درس
6. صعب	5. سهل	4. سؤال
9. ينسى	8. يتذكر	7. إجابة

المدرسة • الدرس

School • Supplies

1. pencil

2. pen

3. crayon

4. backpack

5. paper

6. eraser

7. scissors

8. glue

9. ruler

3. قلم تلوين	2. قلم	1. قلم رصاص
6. ممحاة	5. ورقة	4. حقيبة ظهر
9. مسطرة	8. صمغ	7. مقص

المدرسة • اللوازم

School · Supplies

1. to color
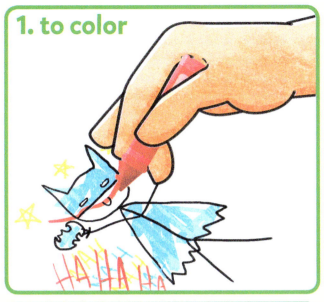

2. to glue

3. to erase

4. to cut

1. يلوّن

2. يلصق

3. يمحي

4. يقص

5. يقيس

5. to measure

School • Computer

1. computer

2. laptop

3. mouse

4. monitor

5. keyboard

6. printer

7. speaker

8. to type

9. to select

3. الفأر	2. حاسوب محمول	1. حاسوب
6. طابعة	5. لوحة المفاتيح	4. شاشة
9. يختار	8. يطبع	7. مكبر صوت

المدرسة • الحاسوب

School • Internet

1. internet

2. website

3. to search

4. username

5. password

6. to log in

7. email

8. to send

9. to download

3. يبحث	2. موقع إلكتروني	1. إنترنت
6. يسجل الدخول	5. كلمة السر	4. اسم المستخدم
9. يقوم بتحميل	8. يرسل	7. بريد إلكتروني

School

1. elementary

2. middle school
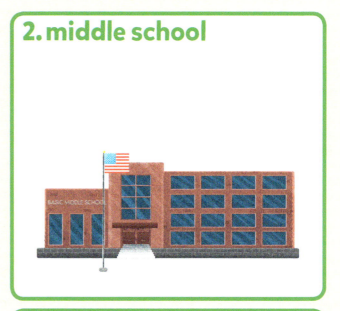

3. high school

4. college
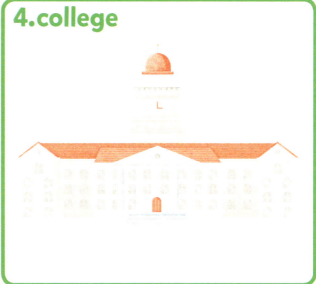

5. school bus

1. ابتدائي

2. المدرسة المتوسطة

3. المدرسة الثانوية

4. كلية

5. باص المدرسة

المدرسة

Chapter 7
City

الفصل 7
المدينة

City

1. city

2. church

3. post office

4. police station

5. fire station

6. city hall

7. airport

8. hospital

9. library

1. مدينة	2. كنيسة	3. مكتب البريد
4. مركز الشرطة	5. محطة الإطفاء	6. قاعة المدينة
7. مطار	8. مستشفى	9. مكتبة

المدينة

City

1. bank

2. museum

3. court house

4. auto shop

5. gas station

6. bus stop

7. parking lot

8. bridge

9. tunnel

3. دار العدل	2. متحف	1. محطة غاز
6. محطة الباص	5. محطة الغاز	4. متجر السيارات
9. نفق	8. جسر	7. موقف

المدينة

City · Car

1. car

2. truck

3. motorcycle

4. semi-truck

5. garbage truck

6. taxi

7. bus

8. train

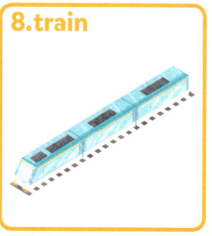

9. subway

3. دراجة نارية	2. شاحنة	1. سيارة
6. سيارة أجرة	5. شاحنة النفايات	4. مقطورة
9. قطار أنفاق	8. قطار	7. حافلة

المدينة • سيارة

City • Car

1. headlight

2. windshield

3. bumper

4. hood

5. license plate

6. tire

7. engine

8. steering wheel

9. gas

1.مصباح أمامي	2.زجاج أمامي	3.ممتص الصدمات
4.قبعة السترة	5.لوحة ترخيص	6.العجلة
7.محرك	8.المقود	9.غاز

City • Traffic

1. traffic

2. traffic light

3. sign

4. intersection

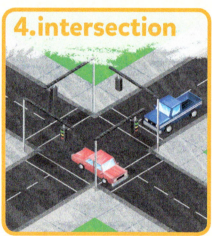

5. corner

6. sidewalk

7. crosswalk

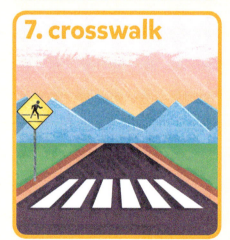

8. street

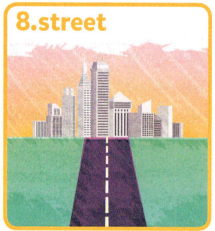

9. highway

3. إشارة	2. إشارة المرور	1. إزدحام
6. رصيف	5. زاوية	4. تقاطع طرق
9. الطريق السريع	8. شارع	7. ممر

City • Traffic

1. to go

2. to stop

3. to cross

4. to get on

5. to get off

6. to wait

7. to drive

8. to park

9. to crash

3. يعبر	2. يتوقف	1. يمرّ
6. ينتظر	5. ينزل	4. يصعد
9. يصطدم	8. يركن	7. يقود

City • Library

1. librarian

2. book

3. magazine

HEALTH MAGAZINE
EATING BEARABLE FOOD
EDIBLE TREE?
FOOD 101!
TEN BEARIFIC RECIPES

4. newspaper

NEWS

5. map

6. title

HEALTH MAGAZINE
EATING BEARABLE FOOD
EDIBLE TREE?
FOOD 101!
TEN BEARIFIC RECIPES

7. to look

8. to get

LIBRAR

9. to return

LIBRAR

3. مجلة	2. كتاب	1. أمين المكتبة
6. عنوان	5. خريطة	4. جريدة
9. يرجع	8. يحصل على	7. ينظر

المدينة • المكتبة

City • Hospital

1. doctor

2. patient

3. ambulance

4. medicine

5. crutch

6. wheelchair

7. injection
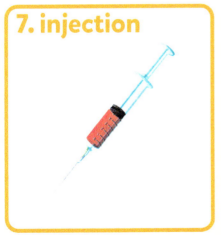

8. cast

9. X-ray

1.طبيب	2.مريض	3. سيارة إسعاف
4.دواء	5.عكاز	6.كرسي متحرك
7. حقنة	8.المصبوب	9.أشعة سينية

المدينة • المستشفى

City • Bank

1. teller

2. money

3. coin

4. check

5. debit card

6. PIN number

7. to deposit

8. to withdraw

9. to save

3. عملة	2. مال	1. أمينة صندوق
6. الرقم السري	5. بطاقة ائتمان	4. شيك
9. يدّخر	8. يسحب	7. يودع

المدينة • البنك

City • Safety

1. police car

2. crime

3. police officer

4. fire truck

5. fire

6. fire fighter

7. airplane

8. passenger

9. pilot

3.ضابط شرطة	2.جريمة	1.سيارة شرطة
6.رجل إطفاء	5.نار	4.سيارة إطفاء
9.طيار	8.راكب	7.مطار

City • Jobs

1. trash collector

2. judge

3. mayor

4. mail carrier

5. driver

6. engineer

7. security

8. architect

9. lawyer

3.عمدة	2.قاضي	1. جامع القمامة
6.مهندس	5.سائق	4.ساعي البريد
9.محامي	8.مهندسة معمارية	7. رجل أمن

المدينة • الوظائف

Chapter 8
Life

الفصل 8
الحياة

Life • Good

1. good

2. quiet

3. smart

4. confident

5. to work

1. حسن
2. هادئ
3. ذكي
4. واثق بنفسه
5. يعمل

الحياة • حسن

Life • Bad

1. bad

2. noisy

3. lazy

4. nervous

5. to steal

1. سيئة
2. صاخبة
3. كسول
4. متوتر
5. يسرق

Life • Store

1. mall

2. store

3. groceries

4. cart

5. line

6. register

7. expensive

8. cheap

9. to buy

3. محلات البقالة	2. متجر	1. مجمع تجاري
6. تسجيل	5. خط	4. عربة التسوق
9. يشتري	8. رخيص	7. غالي

الحياة • متجر

Life • Restaurant

1. chef

2. waiter

3. customer

4. straw

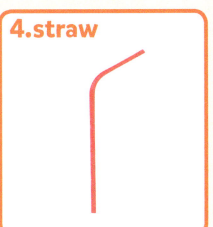

5. lid

6. menu

7. drive-through

8. to order

9. to ask

3. زبون	2. نادل	1. طاهي
6. قائمة الطعام	5. غطاء	4. قشة
9. يسأل	8. يطلب	7. الشراء من السيارة

Life • Phone

1. cell phone

2. to call

3. message

4. camera

5. picture

6. battery

7. to record

8. video

9. to charge

3. رسالة	2. يتصل	1. هاتف خلوي
6. البطارية	5. صورة	4. آلة تصوير
9. يشحن	8. فيديو	7. يسجل

الحياة • هاتف

Life • Music

1. guitar

2. drums

3. piano

4. violin

5. flute
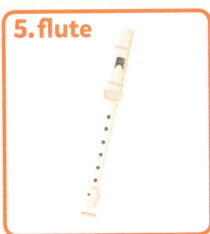

6. trumpet

7. band

8. concert

9. to sing

3. بيانو	2. طبل	1. غيتار
6. بوق	5. مزمار	4. كمان
9. يغني	8. حفلة موسيقية	7. فرقة

الحياة • الموسيقى

Life • Entertainment

1. movie
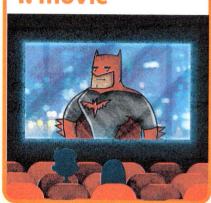

2. show

3. cartoon

4. park

5. bowling

6. arcade
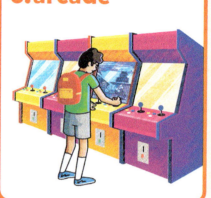

7. zoo

8. roller coaster

9. to ride

3. رسوم متحركة	2. عرض	1. فيلم
6. ممر	5. البولينج	4. منتزه
9. يركب	8. السفينة الدوارة	7. حديقة الحيوانات

الحياة • وسائل الترفيه

Life • Park

1. swing

2. slide

3. monkey bars

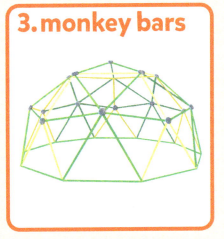

4. bench

5. to run

6. to climb

7. to push

8. to pull

9. to like

3. قضبان أفقية	2. منزلق	1. أراجيح
6. يتسلق	5. يركض	4. مقعد
9. يحب	8. يسحب	7. يدفع

الحياة • منتزه

Life • Sports

1. baseball

2. volleyball

3. basketball

4. football

5. soccer

6. hockey

7. tennis

8. golf

9. cricket

3. كرة السلة	2. الكرة الطائرة	1. البيسبول
6. الهوكي	5. كرة القدم الأمريكية	4. كرة القدم
9. كريكيت	8. جولف	7. تنس

الحياة • الرياضة

Life • Sports

1. surfing

2. snowboarding

3. skating

4. boxing

5. wrestling

6. gymnastics

7. ring

8. stadium

9. track

3.التزلج	2. التزلج على الجليد	1. ركوب الأمواج
6. رياضة بدنية	5. مصارعة	4. ملاكمة
9. حلبة سباق	8. ملعب	7. حلقة

Life • Sports

1. uniform

2. helmet

3. cleats

4. bat

5. goal

6. net

7. to stretch

8. to exercise

9. to practice

3. دبابيس الأحذية	2. خوذة	1. زي موحد
6. شبكة	5. هدف	4. مضرب
9. يتدرّب	8. يتمرن	7. يتمدد

الحياة • الرياضة

Life • Sports

1. to win

2. to lose

3. to score

4. to throw

5. to catch

6. to kick

7. to jump

8. to race

9. to hit

3. يسجل	2. يخسر	1. يفوز
6. يركل	5. يلتقط	4. يرمي
9. يضرب	8. يتسابق	7. يقفز

Life · Sports

1. athlete

2. team

3. coach

4. referee

5. fan

1. رياضي

2. فريق

3. مدرب

4. حكم

5. معجب

الحياة · الرياضة

Chapter 9
Nature

الفصل 9
الطبيعة

Nature • Plants

1. tree

2. bush

3. plant

4. branch

5. leaf

6. root

7. trunk

8. shade

9. to grow

1. شجرة	2. شجيرة	3. نبات
4. فرع شجرة	5. ورقة شجرة	6. جذر
7. جذع	8. ظل	9. ينمو

Nature • Plants

1. cactus

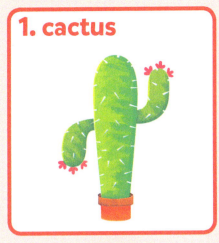

2. palm tree

3. pine tree

4. flower

5. thorn

6. stem

7. seed

8. soil

9. pot

1. صبار	2. شجرة النخيل	3. شجرة الصنوبر
4. زهرة	5. زهرة	6. جذع
7. بذرة	8. تربة	9. وعاء

الطبيعة • النباتات

Nature · Earth

1. Earth

2. land

3. mountain

4. desert
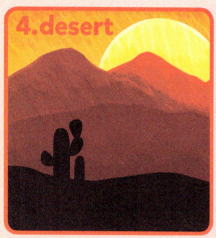

5. jungle

6. forest

7. island

8. hill

9. valley

1. أرض	2. أرض	3. جبل
4. صحراء	5. أدغال	6. غابة
7. جزيرة	8. تلة	9. وادي

الطبيعة • الأرض

Nature • Earth

1. ocean

2. river

3. lake

4. waterfall

5. beach

6. wave

7. mud

8. sand

9. rock

3.بحيرة	2.نهر	1. محيط
6.موجة	5.شاطئ بحر	4.شلال
9.صخرة	8.رمل	7. وحل

الطبيعة • الأرض

129

Nature • Space

1. planet

2. stars

3. comet

4. sun

5. moon

6. satellite

7. astronaut

8. alien
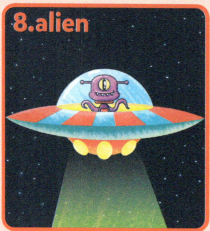

9. to explore

3. مذنب	2. نجمة	1. كوكب
6. قمر صناعي	5. قمر	4. شمس
9. يكتشف	8. كائن فضائي	7. رائد فضاء

Nature · Weather

1. day

2. night

3. morning

4. spring

5. summer

6. afternoon

7. fall

8. winter

9. evening

3. صباح	2. ليل	1. نهار
6. بعد الظهر	5. صيف	4. ربيع
9. مساء	8. شتاء	7. خريف

الطبيعة · الطقس

131

Nature • Weather

1. rain

2. lightning

3. storm

4. sky

5. cloud

6. snow

7. fog

8. puddle

9. umbrella

3.عاصفة	2.برق	1. مطر
6.ثلج	5.غيمة	4.سماء
9.مظلة	8.بركة صغيرة	7. ضباب

Nature • Weather

1. hot

2. warm

3. cold

4. temperature

5. to melt

6. to freeze

7. sunny

8. cloudy

9. windy

3. بارد	2. دافئ	1. حار
6. يجمّد	5. يذوّب	4. حرارة
9. عاصفة	8. غائم	7. مشمس

الطبيعة • الطقس

Nature • Environment

1. tornado

2. volcano

3. tidal wave

4. hurricane

5. flood

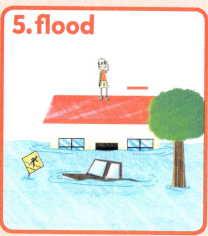

6. avalanche

7. wildfire

8. drought

9. earthquake

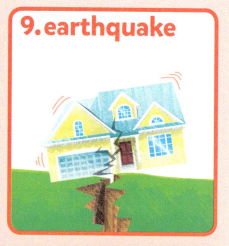

1. زوبعة	2. بركان	3. المد والجزر
4. إعصار	5. فيضان	6. انهيار ثلجي
7. حريق هائل	8. جفاف	9. زلزال

الطبيعة • البيئة

Nature • Environment

1. to help

2. to rescue

3. to take

4. to give

5. to share

1. يساعد

2. ينقذ

3. يأخذ

4. يعطي

5. يشارك

الطبيعة • البيئة

Nature • Environment

1. to recycle

2. to litter

3. to use

4. to waste

5. pollution

1. يعيد تدوير

2. يرمي القمامة

3. يستخدم

4. يهدر

5. تلوث

الطبيعة • البيئة

Chapter 10
Animals

الفصل 10
الحيوانات

Animals • Farm

1. cow

2. pig

3. chicken

4. donkey

5. horse

6. turkey

7. goat

8. sheep

9. farm

1. بقرة	2. خنزير	3. دجاجة
4. حمار	5. حصان	6. ديك رومي
7. معزاة	8. خروف	9. مزرعة

الحيوانات • المزرعة

Animals • Ocean

1. fish 	2. shark 	3. squid 
4. octopus 	5. crab 	6. whale 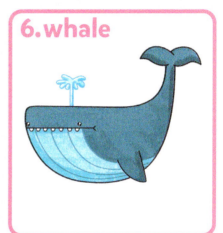
7. dolphin 	8. seal 	9. to swim 

3. حبار	2. قرش	1. سمك
6. حوت	5. سلطعون	4. أخطبوط
9. يسبح	8. فقمة	7. دولفين

Animals • Forest

1. bear

2. raccoon

3. porcupine

4. deer

5. skunk

6. wolf

7. fur

8. cave

9. to howl

1. دب	2.الظربان الأمريكي	3.قنفذ
4.غزال	5.الظربان الأمريكي	6.ذئب
7. فرو	8.كهف	9.يعوي

الحيوانات • الغابة

Animals • Jungle

1. panda

2. lion

3. crocodile

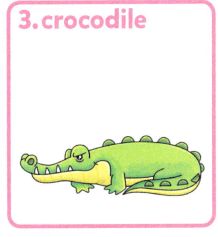

4. monkey

5. elephant

6. snake

7. giraffe

8. zebra

9. camel

3.تمساح	2.أسد	1. دب الباندا
6.حية	5.فيل	4.قرد
9.جمل	8.حمار وحشي	7. زرافة

Animals • Birds

1. bird

2. wing

3. beak

4. feather

5. claw
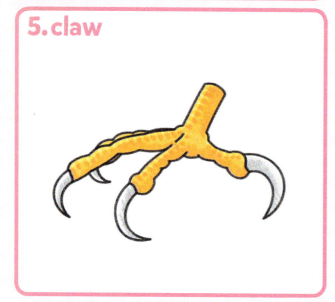

1. عصفور

2. جناح

3. منقار

4. ريشة

5. مخلب

الحيوانات • الطيور

Animals • Birds

1. eagle

2. owl

3. duck

4. penguin

5. peacock

6. hummingbird

7. flamingo

8. nest

9. to fly

3.بطة	2.بومة	1. نسر
6.طائر الطنان	5.الطاووس	4.بطريق
9.يطير	8.عش	7. طائر مائي

Animals • Pets

1. dog

2. puppy

3. lizard

4. cat

5. kitten

6. frog

7. rabbit

8. goldfish

9. turtle
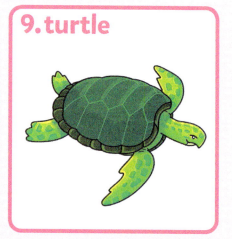

1. كلب	2. جرو	3. سحلية
4. قطة	5. قطة صغيرة	6. ضفدع
7. أرنب	8. ذهبية	9. سلحفاة

الحيوانات • الحيوانات الأليفة

Animals • Pets

1. leash

2. collar

3. aquarium

4. cage

5. to feed

6. to pet

7. to chase

8. to train

9. to walk

3. حوض سمك	2. طوق	1. سلسة
6. يدلل	5. يطعم	4. قفص
9. يمشي	8. يدرّب	7. يطارد

Animals • Insects

1. bee

2. mosquito
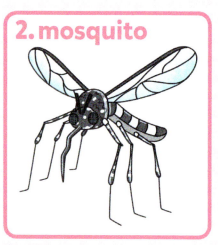

3. fly
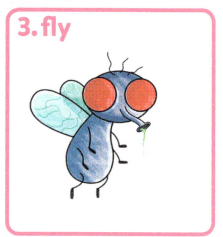

4. butterfly

5. spider

6. web

7. ant

8. snail

9. shell

3. ذبابة	2. بعوض	1. نحلة
6. شبكة	5. عنكبوت	4. فراشة
9. صدف	8. حلزون	7. نملة

الحيوانات • الحشرات

Glossary

Glossary

C

المعجم

Glossary

D

Glossary

المعجم

Glossary

Glossary

المعجم

Glossary

Glossary

O

P

المعجم

Glossary

Q

R

S

Glossary

المعجم

Glossary

T

المعجم

Glossary

المعجم

Glossary

المعجم